# YOU'VE BEEN DRINKING MUDDY WATER
# AND OTHER SOUTHERN TALES

© 2024 Alison Large Ketcham

All rights reserved. This book contains material protected under International and Federal Copyright Laws and Treaties. Any unauthorized reprint or use of this material is prohibited. No part of this book may be reproduced, distributed, or transmitted in any form or by any means, including photocopying, recording, or other electronic or mechanical means, without the prior written permission of the author.

We all have stories. After all, that's what life is, a series of stories. Most of us probably have enough to fill a book. The hard part is writing them all down and creating that book.

That's what I've done here – I have written down some of my stories – which might not be all that different from yours.

If you've made it this far, I hope you read on. And I hope you enjoy what you read. Maybe some of these stories will make you smile, reflect on happy times, and hopefully even laugh.

Whether you're reading this on the beach, in bed, at a coffee shop, or in the bathroom, thanks for being here.

## Table of Contents

1. You've Been Drinking Muddy Water ................ 1
2. Killing Snakes ................ 7
3. Riding Shotgun & Shooting Ducks ................ 13
4. Best Friends ................ 18
5. He Went to the Back of the Bus Anyway ................ 25
6. Heebie & Jeebie ................ 30
7. Ziggy Stardust the Goat ................ 36
8. Where's Joe? ................ 42
9. Alison with One "L" ................ 48
10. Catching Yawns ................ 52
11. Shakin' a Tower ................ 55
12. The Tooth Fairy? ................ 59
13. Doppelgänger ................ 62
14. Uncle Bill ................ 65
15. Fruit Flies ................ 69
16. Online Dating ................ 73
17. Spiders vs. Roaches ................ 79
18. Catching Up To Do ................ 84

For my kids Zeke and Johnathan; step kids Putter and Beanie; cousins Patty, Susan and Billy, and special fella Benny. Thanks for making my life immeasurably richer.

# You've Been Drinking Muddy Water

"Billy, you've been drinking muddy water," my grandmother said to my 12-year-old cousin as he stood slap-dab in front of the TV, captivated by The Jackson Five performing on the Ed Sullivan Show.

"What does that mean?" I asked Diddledee, as we heard Michael, the youngest of the Jackson brothers, singing "Oh baby give me one more chance," through the Zenith speakers, and Cousin Billy stepped aside.

It was a Sunday evening in the late 1960s, and our family was gathered around the TV in the den of Diddledee's Craftsman-style home in Albany, Georgia. I'd probably heard my grandmother talk about drinking muddy water before. But at eight years old, this was the first time the words registered.

"Why did you say Billy's been drinking muddy water?" I asked again, not having a clue.

"Because we can't see through him," Diddledee laughed.

"Oh," I exclaimed. "Now I get it!"

Fifty-plus years later, my cousins and I still say "You've been drinking muddy water" if someone stands in front of a TV. Some of our kids do too.

Diddledee, who was my mama's mama, was the sweetest person I've ever known. Born Neva Lynn Balthrop in 1895, as an adult she stood 4-feet-11-inches tall and never weighed more than 100 pounds soaking wet.

Her silky gray hair hung to her waist when not pulled up in a bird's-nest bun. Rumor revealed she hadn't had more than a trim since World War II. She brushed her silky mane 100 strokes nightly and each morning secured the nest with twists and brown bobby pins.

She was a constant in our lives until she died in 1979, leaving countless memories — and sayings — for me and my cousins.

"Dog take it," Diddledee once said when she realized she had put too much detergent in the laundromat washing machine and bubbles cascaded to the floor. With the help of an attendant, a bucket, and a couple of small trash cans, we scooped up the mess, mopped and finished our loads. "At least now we know the floor's clean!" she concluded.

"Saints be amazed!" Diddledee responded gleefully when I showed her my second-grade report card filled with A's and only one B. "I never doubted you could do it for a second."

"Will wonders never cease?" she said when one after another, her grandchildren performed flips, jack knives, and can openers off the diving board of our backyard pool. "Every one of y'all is amazing!"

"Home again, home again, jiggity jig," Diddledee said every time we pulled into her gravel driveway after a trip to the laundromat, Pak-A-Sak, or pet store (for me to get one more green snake).

"Land sakes alive!" Diddledee said when I was three years old and told her I had broken my arm when I slid it backwards through the back of a stretchy lawn chair.

A few days later, a typed poem and her illustration of me in a cast arrived in the mail.

"There was a little girl
    And I am not a jokin'.
There was a little girl
    Whose little arm was broken.

The doctor said to her
    'Let's make a caster of plaster.'
And that is what they did
    To make her arm well faster.

Now let's play a game
    Of guessing what's her name.
This lovey dovey one
    Is my sweet Alison."

My grandmother smelled of Vick's VapoRub and VO5. She drank Sanka instant coffee and collected Top Value Stamps. She spent countless hours playing Rummy and Hide-the-Thimble with her grandchildren. And because she kept forgetting the name of the new "less messy" canned pasta, she called them Spiro Agnews instead of SpaghettiOs.

A few Christmases ago, I framed black-and-white prints of the wagon-wheel trellis which stood forever at the end of my grandmother's sweeping front porch. Our parents sold her house shortly after Diddledee died, so it's been a long time since any of us have seen the trellis in person. Her house is now abandoned, and the trellis long gone.

I watched as two of my Atlanta cousins opened their trellis-picture presents and smiled as they each became misty. I mailed another to Cousin Billy in Houston who called, gushed, and said he was going to find a special place in his home for it.

It says a lot about a person that their grandchildren still become teary thinking about them more-than 40 years after their death. I hope I leave that kind of loving legacy for my grandchildren, some of whom are yet to be born. And I hope I will be able to look down and know I've done so.

Then I hope I can turn to Diddledee and thank her for setting a high bar. She was as close to perfect as a mortal can be. I guess you could say she was as pure as the driven snow.

Even when she'd been drinking muddy water.

*Cousins in the mid-1960s at grandmother Diddledee's Albany, Georgia home. Alison is seated on the left with cousins Billy and Patty. Cousin Cindy is standing on the left next to Alison's sister Lisa.*

*Diddledee and Alison in the early-1960s at Radium Springs Gardens in Albany, Georgia.*

*The wagon wheel trellis that anchored one end of Diddledee's porch for decades.*

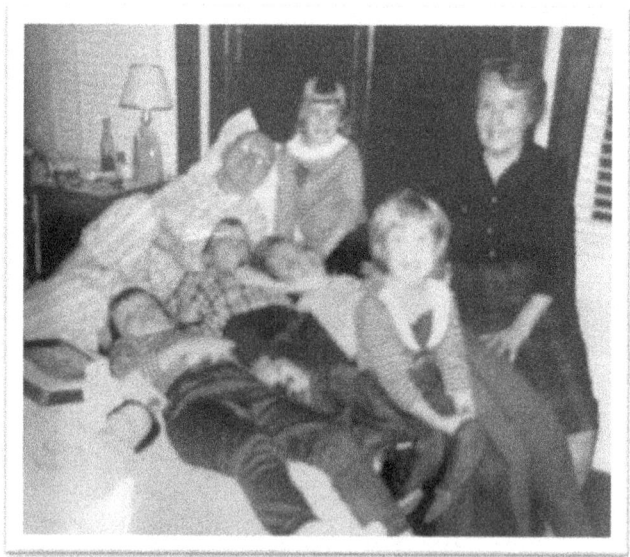

*Alison, with her sister Lisa and cousins Billy, Cindy and Patty posing for a picture in the '60s with their granddaddy and Diddledee.*

## Killing Snakes

I never questioned whether everybody's daddy stopped to kill snakes on the way to and from the beach. Mine did though.

And I never questioned why.

It was the 1960s, and my family made regular trips from Birmingham to Destin, Florida to fish, crab, play in the surf, eat fresh seafood, and make memories.

Some of those memories include my father killing snakes off the side of U.S. Highway 331.

"Nancy, please stop so I can kill a snake," my father E. Ray Large would say to my mother between beer sips as we were hoofing it toward the coast for a few carefree days in the sun. "I need you to pull over."

There was always a sense of urgency to my father's need to kill snakes. He would ask Mama to pull over quickly, as though taking too much time might dampen his ability to annihilate a particular leg-less reptile in the woods alongside the highway

My sister Lisa and I would be in the back of our light-blue four-door Buick, more than likely joined by a couple of friends or cousins along for the adventure. Lisa is four years older than me, and at the time we were both younger than 10.

"OK Ray," Mama would say in her sweet South Georgia drawl. "I'm pulling over as fast as I can."

Daddy would open the passenger door, set his beer can on the floorboard, stand up on the gravel shoulder, and strike off to the tree line. He'd disappear into the pines for a few minutes before coming back declaring success.

"I killed a big one, y'all," Daddy would say as he picked up his Budweiser and settled back into the passenger seat. "Used the biggest stick I could find."

"Yay Daddy," we'd erupt while bouncing on the backseat. "You killed that mean old snake!"

Sometimes Daddy would just kill one snake per trip down or back. Sometimes he'd kill two. Occasionally he'd feel the urge to kill three. He'd come back reciting how big the snake was, how hard it was to fight, and ultimately how he spared the world of one more evil menace.

I never asked why though. I never questioned the efficiency of pulling off the road to kill snakes when we were hurrying to the beach or home. I was just the proud daughter of a man who killed snakes.

One Sunday afternoon, we were heading back from several days of fun in the sun to get ready for the upcoming school and work week.

"Nancy, I need to kill one," Daddy said.

"OK Ray," Mama replied, crunching to a gravely stop.

Daddy disappeared into the tree line, then reappeared a few minutes later. This time carrying a prop.

We all watched through rolled-down windows as he held up a two-foot-long stick as big around as a baseball bat, and announced that was the weapon he had just used to kill the biggest snake so far.

"Wow, Daddy!" I said, not even trying to control my excitement. "How big was the snake?"

"About twice as long as this stick," he said. "I really had to fight hard. But I did it."

From that moment on, I was determined to take that stick to show-and-tell the next day at Mother Goose Kindergarten.

Mama and Daddy agreed.

"Sure, you can take the stick to school tomorrow," Daddy said. "That would make me proud."

I wish now I had a recording of the conversation my parents had that night after my sister and I were tucked away in our beds. Now that I'm older — and somewhat wiser — I imagine it went something like this:

"Ray, the girls really believe you are killing snakes," Mama probably said. "They have no idea you are actually stopping to tee-tee."

"I know, Nancy," Daddy probably replied. "But they get so excited, I don't want to change the story now. Who knows? In 30 years, they'll probably tell their kids about how their Ol' Dad used to kill snakes on the way to and from the beach.

"Alison might even write a story about it."

The next morning, I proudly stood in front of my class, holding up the stick my Daddy used to kill a snake.

"Wow, what a brave Daddy you have," one girl said.

"I wish my Daddy would stop and kill snakes on the way home from the beach," a little boy exclaimed.

I stood a little taller from that day forward, prouder than ever to be my Daddy's daughter. And nobody was the wiser — least of all me.

*Alison's mama and daddy, Nancy and E. Ray Large, having fun on a Destin, Florida beach in the early 1970s.*

*Alison on the left and her sister Lisa on the right in Destin, Florida in the 1960s.*

Alison's daddy wearing a straw hat on a Destin beach in the 1960s.

Alison's mama in the late 1960s.

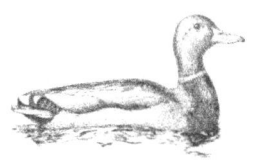

# Riding Shotgun & Shooting Ducks

I doubt it was legal even back then. On the other hand, no one probably ever considered a law against it. Who would be crazy enough to shoot a duck from the front seat of a Toyota anyway?

Well, I would.

Forty-five years later, I still rib Cousin Susan she made me do it. Instructing me that early Mississippi morning to turn backward in the passenger seat of her white '78 Corolla, thrust a double-barrel 12-gauge out the window, set sights on a mallard paddling a football field or so away, and pull the trigger.

We were on our way to duck hunt anyway, 20-year-old Susan figured. So why not a little pre-game action? Who would have guessed the only one in the car who hadn't ever shot an animal would score the first touchdown?

Susan was behind the wheel on our way to hunt. Her cousin Karla and Karla's fiancé Bowen were in the back seat.

We had Jon boats, camo blinds, and decoys waiting in our swampy-water destination. A smattering of duck calls, barrels aimed at the sky, and a measure of patience would round out the recipe.

En route, though, Susan whipped to the gravel shoulder and ground to a noisy halt. She spotted a flock of mallards atop a small lake and instructed me to do my part.

I obliged.

"Woohoo," the car erupted when the splash died down. "You killed it!"

I was 18 at the time. Karla and Bowen were 20 like Susan. Hunting was a way of life for them. Plucking feathers, skinning rabbits, and dressing deer came as natural as snapping peas, shucking corn, and four-wheeling through mud puddles.

I was a raised-in-the-city fisherman myself, but an outdoors lover, nonetheless. Susan's invite to ride shotgun to Greenwood and try my hand at hunting, drinking beer, and four-wheeling through mud puddles sounded like a blast.

But after the shot heard 'round the Toyota, I quickly realized hunting was not a blast for me after all.

Bowen slid out of the car, slipped waders over his camos and headed to the lake. He returned carrying a beautiful brown-and-cream hen with orange webbed feet and brilliant-blue feathers punctuating each wing.

I wanted to cry.

He laid her on my lap, and I could feel the warmth her body hadn't yet released. My mind reeled. What right did I have to rob this beautiful creature of life? I had never even eaten duck, and from what I heard, I wasn't missing anything.

And what if she had left babies behind?

Eating what one kills is the rationale for hunting. And I'd be lying if I said I'm not a carnivore. I can savor a grilled ribeye, baked pork chop, or deep-fried chicken breast with the best of them. But I realized that day I never again wanted to be directly responsible for the death of an animal.

Call it hypocrisy, denial, whatever you want, but them's the facts. At my age it's not likely I'm going to go all vegetarian, but I also have never again snuck up on an animal and whisked away its shot at life. Nor do I plan to.

No, I prefer my meat prepackaged and plucked from a fridge. And I don't think about what the cuts looked like when they were still part of a whole.

But I don't hold hunting against anyone else either.

"That," my beloved father would say, "falls under the heading of their business."

I have, however, and will continue to tell — with remorse — the story of the one time I downed a duck. And maybe, just maybe, my experience will influence a potential hunter to take up crocheting or pole vaulting.

It was back when I was young and game for almost anything adventurous. When I thought hunting would be a welcome addition to my repertoire. Before I found out making a wild animal go limp would break my heart.

Back when — that one time — I gave it a shot. From the front seat of a Toyota.

*Alison's cousin Susan riding a three-wheeler at Cousin Karla's after duck hunting.*

*Cousin Susan after falling off the three-wheeler while popping wheelies.*

*Cousin Karla popping wheelies on a three-wheeler after the duck hunt.*

*Karla apparently enjoying falling off the three-wheeler.*

## Best Friends

One of many great men my father was friends with when I was a child was named Ulysses — like America's 18th President.

It was the 1960s in racially turbulent Birmingham, Alabama, and my father E. Ray Large and Ulysses Gholston became friends on an elevator.

Our Ulysses' didn't pronounce his name the way Ulysses S. Grant did though.

Grant's first name was enunciated "U-liss-sis," emphasis on "liss."

Our Ulysses' name was pronounced "You-la-seize," emphasis on "You."

There was another distinct difference between our Ulysses and Ulysses S. Grant (aside from the fact that they lived in different centuries). Grant was a man whose skin we call "white" and our Ulysses' skin color is typically called "black."

My Daddy's skin color was white as was my mother's, my sister's and mine.

Our Ulysses came into my family's life when he was working as an elevator operator in downtown Birmingham's Massey Building.

Back then, crisply clad men manned many office-building elevators, and in gestures akin to a butler's or chauffeur's, asked riders which floor they were bound for, dialed the circular clock-like handle to the corresponding number, then delivered their passengers one by one.

At the time, my father was a young, ambitious attorney working on The Massey Building's third floor, riding up and down its elevator daily, bound for — or returning from — the county courthouse, a local cafeteria, or a round or two of handball at the downtown YMCA.

Call it fate or call it serendipity that placed these two strapping young men routinely in the same place at the same time, but that elevator provided a platform for the seeds of a lifelong friendship, as well as an example for me of how skin-color variations only make life richer.

Not that my family gave a flip about Ulysses' skin color. I remember asking my mother when I was 10 years old, and we lived down the road from the epicenter of the Civil Rights Movement, what she would say if I wanted to marry a black man when I grew up.

"I would just want to know you loved him," sweet Mama said in her melodic South Georgia drawl. No hesitation, no debate.

That set the tone for my life. My parents taught me that skin color matters no more than hair or eye color when it comes to things that are truly important — the value of a life, the kindness of a person, the respect we show others, the content of one's character. No hesitation, no debate.

Our Ulysses was born in 1940 in Sumter County, Alabama, a place known for endless fields of clover; woodlands popping with deer, turkey and raccoons; ponds and lakes filled with gargantuan largemouth bass and translucent yellow-bellied bream; and winding two-lane roads leading pretty-much nowhere.

In those days, Sumter County was also known as a place where more often than not there was a stark contrast between the quality of life for whites and blacks, with whites usually coming out on top.

I haven't been to Sumter County in more-than 10 years, when I attended Ulysses' funeral, held in an overflowing white-clapboard church alongside one of those winding roads still leading nowhere.

I would like to think the contrast between black and white lives is no longer stark in Sumter County, or anywhere else across this country, although I know it's not always true. At Ulysses' funeral in 2011, though, blacks and whites sat and stood side by side celebrating and crying together over the life of a kind, accomplished man. No one cared if his skin had been black or white. Why would we?

Back in the '60s, my father's and Ulysses' friendship moved beyond the elevator when Daddy asked Ulysses if he would trim dozens of Cherry Laurel trees lining our backyard. My parents weren't wealthy but had the forethought in '61, when they bought our modest gray-brick house on a cul-de-sac, to also purchase the lot next door to one day expand our footprint.

A few years later, they had a gray-metal fence installed around the perimeter of both lots — to keep kids and dogs corralled — then anchored it with thick pine-straw beds and a wall of Cherry Laurels.

Ulysses accepted Daddy's offer and began trimming our Cherry Laurels on the weekends to supplement his elevator-job income. Over time, Daddy — who had his hands full establishing a law practice — asked Ulysses for help with other tasks: sealing a notch knocked out of a pine tree struck by lightning, capturing a massive hornets' nest outside my sister's bedroom window, tending to our soft St. Augustine grass to keep it healthy north of its native habitat, and planting shrubs and flowers around the yard.

Over time, friends saw Ulysses' meticulous work and began hiring him to trim their trees, and more. Before long, Ulysses and Daddy drew up corporation papers establishing Gholston Tree Service. From then on, Ulysses' sky was the limit.

He hired crews, had trucks emblazoned with the Gholston name, and took on almost more business than he could handle. But even while managing his thriving company, Ulysses always came back in his mustard-yellow pickup to carefully trim our Cherry Laurels.

Years passed. Daddy became a well-respected trial attorney, moved a block south into the esteemed City Federal Building, and served in the mid '70s as president of the Birmingham Bar Association. Always the entrepreneurial type, he turned down several offers from bigger firms to keep charting his own course.

Then in 1982, when my beloved Mama was 54, she was diagnosed with liposarcoma, a rare form of soft-tissue cancer. Mama bravely endured seven major surgeries, radiation and chemo treatments, keeping the cancer at bay for nine years — well beyond her oncologist's early prognosis.

"Your Mama just had major surgery," her doctor said. "And she's going to a dinner party Friday night.

"You tell me why she's still alive."

We were all heartbroken in February '91 when Mama succumbed to the cancer. But over time, Daddy bucked up publicly by pouring himself into his beloved law practice, taking time off to travel and fish, and even dating. Still, though, Mama was the love of his life, and her absence left an unfillable void.

In January 2001, just shy of a decade after Mama's death, Daddy had a fatal heart attack and was found the next day on the floor of his home for 40 years, the gray-brick house on a cul-de-sac surrounded by silky St. Augustine grass, deep pine-straw beds, and deeply rooted Cherry Laurel trees.

We were all stunned and heartbroken, as Daddy was only 73 and had won two games of rooftop handball the day he died. But a friend summarized his life well through tears at Daddy's visitation the night before the funeral.

"He got every drop there was to get out of life and then he dropped dead," the friend said. "We should all be so lucky."

A few months later, I was at the house sorting through lifetimes of belongings, intermittently crying and smiling. As I carried a load to the garage, Ulysses and his sweet wife Aurelia pulled up in front of the house. We hugged and shared how much we all missed Daddy.

As tears welled, Ulysses — with graying temples and not as tall and strapping as I remembered — said something I will never forget.

"I haven't bought my own socks since 1967," he said, tears spilling down his cheeks. "Your daddy always bought my socks."

I didn't ask Ulysses why Daddy bought his socks all those years. I guess I didn't want to seem disrespectful looking into the crying face of a man I loved.

I sometimes wish I had, as I have reflected on that conversation countless times. Now it's too late to know for sure. On the other hand, I believe I do know the answer — because of my father's character, and the depth of his and Ulysses' friendship.

I believe early on my father figured buying Ulysses socks was a way to help his friend, as operating an elevator probably paid less than even a young attorney made. The gesture became a habit, and even after Ulysses was running a thriving business, my father wanted him to know he had Ulysses' back.

Daddy never told me — or anyone else I know of — that he gifted those socks all those years. For me that makes the act even more meaningful.

It also confirms what I learned by example many years ago, that skin color is the least characteristic by which we should judge. And in fact, by doing so, we could forego some of the best relationships we'd ever have.

Thanks Daddy and Ulysses for your wonderful example. I can't wait until the day I can hug you both again.

*Alison's daddy E. Ray Large and his friend Ulysses Gholston at her dad's 70th birthday party.*

*Ulysses Gholston and his wife Aurelia.*

# He Went to the Back of the Bus Anyway

Gustava Hollis began working as my father's secretary in 1960, a couple of months before I was born. She retired 40 years later, having helped my daddy, E. Ray Large, build a thriving law practice and win several big jury trials.

Gus was a smart, sweet country girl, the oldest of 12 children raised on a farm in Cullman County, up I-65 an hour or so north of Birmingham. She also just happened to be white.

Daddy died of a heart attack six months after Gus retired. Mama had died of cancer 10 years earlier, and after that a lot of what made life enjoyable for Daddy was gone. He still loved his family beyond measure, but I remember him saying "Old age makes tragedy of too long a life."

That explained a lot.

Gus was a dear friend and a big part of my formative years. Her Christian faith and unassuming nature were something to behold. After her husband Charles died of a heart attack when they were in their 40s, I asked Gus why they never had children.

"Charles said he would tell me when he was ready," she replied. "And he never said he was."

On another occasion I asked Gus why she rarely brought up her faith.

"I don't need to," she said. "God knows."

Not that she wouldn't share when asked. She was instrumental in me developing the Christian beliefs I still hold. But she never wanted her devotion to be perceived as anything but authentic.

A friend, client, and frequent visitor to my father's law office in the '60s was Ulysses Gholston, a kind, accomplished man my father met in downtown Birmingham's Massey Building where Ulysses was an elevator operator. Ulysses was born in rural Sumter County, a couple of hours southwest of Birmingham on the Mississippi line. He just happened to be black.

I always knew growing up how much Gus and Ulysses meant to my family, but it wasn't until years later that I realized how much they meant to each other.

Gus shared a story one day that reminded me skin color doesn't matter when it comes to matters of the heart. It doesn't matter in any other way either. It's just a variation in pigmentation.

One steamy summer afternoon, at the end of a long workday in the mid-1960s, Gus and Ulysses left the office headed to a nearby bus stop to catch eastbound rides home. After Ulysses walked Gus to the door at the front of the bus, he turned to head to the door at the back.

"I said 'Ulysses,'" Gus recalled. "'You don't have to do that.'

"This was long after Rosa Parks," she continued, referring to the black civil rights icon who in the 1950s refused to move to the back of a Montgomery, Alabama bus to give her seat to a white man, setting off a cascade of events leading to a 1956 federal-court decision that forced-segregation on a bus is unconstitutional.

From that point on, no person ever again should have to sit in a certain place on a bus because of skin color.

"Ulysses turned back to me, and said 'Yes ma'am, I do,'" Gus said. "And I know he did it for me. He didn't want anyone — white or black — to judge me for getting on the bus with a black man."

"So he humbled himself for your sake, even though he didn't have to?" I asked.

"Without question," Gus said.

Once inside the bus, Gus and Ulysses didn't sit together either, which is a tragedy.

I don't know if the two of them ever discussed what happened that day, although I can't imagine Gus wouldn't have celebrated Ulysses for such a selfless act. I am certain she told my father as she would have known how moved he would be.

But even if Gus and Ulysses never discussed that day, they both knew what happened.

God knows too. And that's all that really matters.

*One of Alison's father's best friends, Ulysses Gholston.*

*Alison and her daddy's secretary Gustava "Gus" Hollis having dinner in the late 1980s at John's Restaurant in Birmingham.*

## Heebie & Jeebie

Critters like to roam the woods behind my home.

The other night, one of those critters tried to invite himself in. Unfortunately for me, he missed the lesson on how to ring doorbells.

I knew something was awry when I was rudely awakened at 2 a.m. by loud scratching on the window screen near my headboard. I was scared to death to draw back the curtain. What if I found myself face to face with a burglar? But what if I laid there instead and gave said burglar time to break in?

I opted to take my chances and peek. As I slowly pulled back the curtain, I found myself looking straight into the eyes of a bandit. A four-legged one with a mask and ringed tail.

A raccoon.

I still am not sure what Rocky's intent was, but his hooked claws were doing a number on my screen. Pinholes gave way to quarter-size tears.

My cat Callie heard the scratching too and joined me at the window.

Before long, our wannabe intruder realized the two of us were staring back at him, nosedived off the windowsill, and half-waddled, half-ran under a Harvest Moon back into the woods.

Raccoons are cute animals from a distance, or when they have been hand raised and are accustomed to humans. They'll perch on the sofa and play with your hair like they're digging through pine straw for grub worms.

With training, they can even learn to do tricks like Fido such as rolling over, shaking hands, and high fiving. But they lose some of their charm when they're tearing holes in your screen in the middle of the night.

The most I have been around a raccoon was when I was a teenager, and Cousin Susan came home from a Mississippi trip with a baby one named Heebie.

For nearly a year, Susan took Heebie with her everywhere. He blossomed from a one-pound kit to a 30-pound adult, perpetually perched on Susan's shoulder, enjoying bird's-eye views of the world around him.

"He went with me everywhere," Susan smiled. "Back then there weren't rules keeping animals out of stores, so I'd take him to the mall with me." When, on occasion, Heebie did climb down from Susan's shoulder, he loved swatting ice cubes around an aluminum pan until they melted, then marveling over where they'd gone. Another favorite was playing with bream in a bucket brought home from a fishing trip.

Susan fed her masked buddy dog food, fruit, and leftover fishing minnows.

But as a wise man (surely) once said, "You can take the animal out of the wild, but you can't take the wild out of the animal."

After a year of domestic bliss with Susan, nature was calling Heebie pretty loudly, luring him out of his pen and up trees in the yard, making it nearly impossible for even Susan to coax him back down.

Then one day, he got out of the pen and headed down the street to a wooded creek.

"The call of the wild got him," Susan laughed. "He went on a search for his woman."

And find his woman, Heebie did. A few months later, he and his new bride set up house in a tree in Susan's family's front yard.

"He raised a family in that big old oak tree in front of Mama and Daddy's house," Susan recalled. "That summer there were three babies sticking their heads out of that tree."

By then, Susan and the rest of the family were content to see Heebie from a distance. Just knowing he was alive and happy was enough.

Although he spent the rest of his life in the suburban wild, Heebie didn't start out that way. His domestication began when Susan and her cousin Karla got Heebie and littermate Jeebie from a raccoon breeder in rural Mississippi.

They'd made arrangements to buy the two freshly weaned kits to raise as pets, but when they arrived at the breeder's farm, the breeder wasn't home.

"Karla's fiancé reached into a cage of babies and took two anyway," Susan laughed. "We were kids and got caught up in the moment. Karla and I were back in the truck ready to go, Bowen handed us each a raccoon, then jumped in and we sped off.

"'Y'all look like you've got the heebie jeebies,' Bowen laughed at the time," Susan said. "The names stuck, and that's the story."

While Susan brought Heebie back to Alabama, Karla welcomed Jeebie into the family's Mississippi branch.

"I sure miss that rascal," Karla laughed recently. "He loved running up the back of a chair with someone sitting in it, pouncing on their head, and scaring them to death. Especially my great-grandmother.

"Then she would scream 'Damn, get this coon off me!'

"Granddaddy always kept peppermints in his pocket for Jeebie, and Jeebie knew it. He would wait for my grandfather to sit in his chair, run up the back of the chair, get on his shoulder and run his paws into his pocket."

Just like Heebie, Jeebie escaped about a year after liberation from the breeder, living out the rest of his days in the Mississippi backwoods.

Heebie spent the rest of his life on Birmingham's Shades Mountain, happily populating the area with an untold number of baby raccoons.

The house on Shades Mountain where Susan's family and Heebie lived is about five miles from my home, so I like to think the critter ripping holes in my screen that night was one of Heebie's descendants.

Maybe he had a hankering for a pan of ice cubes, or maybe he'd seen a rod and reel through the window and wondered if I had any minnows.

Or maybe he just wanted me to tell Susan hello.

Consider it done, little buddy. Consider it done.

*Alison and her cousin Susan Large Ogletree in the 1960s.*

*Cousin Susan Large Ogletree's raccoon Heebie perched atop her back in the 1970s.*

# Ziggy Stardust the Goat

Hopefully the statute of limitations has run on criminal charges for stealing a goat from a monastery in the 1970s.

But if not, what would the charges be?

Admittedly stealing is a crime, and lifting a goat over the fence around a monastery qualifies as such, but wouldn't the act be forgiven when the childhood friends who took said goat returned it after it started foaming at the mouth and got its horns stuck in my family's brick chimney?

Now, I'd like to be perfectly clear. I did not steal the goat from the monastery. No offense to the boys who did – or their parents – but my parents taught me better. As recently as last week, in fact, I walked back into Whole Foods and used self-checkout to pay for a candy bar I discovered at the bottom of my buggy when I was loading groceries into my car.

Granted, I did do some things in my teens that neither my parents – nor I – were proud of, and I regret those things to this day. But my sweet mama and daddy apparently planted my moral compass deep, because at some point it usurped my childish impulses, and I still rely on it for guidance decades later.

No, I didn't steal the goat that ended up briefly in my backyard and that we named Ziggy Stardust. A couple of my wayward teenage friends did. But in their defense, many kids in the '70s were prone to "mischief." And at the time, mischief was probably what those boys considered lifting a goat from a monastery to be. The word "stealing" likely never entered their minds. I assume they were out riding around, saw the herd of goats doing what goats do, and thought "Why not?"

After all, we didn't have cell phones, social media, or video games, and were only on the cusp of cable TV. As a matter of fact, in a lot of ways, we were better off. We spent more time outdoors, riding bikes, swimming, splashing in creeks, climbing trees, playing hide-and-seek and kick the can, and trying to catch birds with Styrofoam coolers propped up with sticks tied to strings.

But as our collective lot advanced to our mid-teens and started driving, we began spending a lot of time riding around in cars, gathering in parking lots, and generally getting into mischief. The world from behind the steering wheel of a '75 Ford Granada or a '76 Toyota Celica was our oyster. We were limited only by curfews and our allegiance to promises to our parents. No phone tracking, no Ring Doorbells, and a general don't-ask-don't-tell policy.

When my friends (whom I will keep anonymous) found themselves loading a tri-color billy goat into the backseat of a parent's Chevy Suburban, it wasn't long before they questioned what to do with said goat. Once the adrenaline rush of taking the goat lessened, reality probably began taunting them with questions like "What do we feed him?" and "Where are we going to keep him?"

To keep the adrenaline-rush alive, this duo of miscreants first took Ziggy to Bienville, a neighborhood near my childhood home where lots of our friends lived. And as the trio of two teens and a goat wheeled up in front of one of our friend's houses where kids gathered, the boys probably got just the response they were seeking.

"Where the heck did y'all get that goat?" one of our friends asked.

"You're not going to believe this…" one of the boys replied.

From there, I am sure Ziggy was unloaded from the back seat and petted and cooed over by at least a dozen kids. Hopefully, it was a good experience for Ziggy as I have no idea whether he was accustomed to being surrounded by humans, or whether he had ridden in a back seat before. I am assuming probably "no" to both.

Then, I am sure reality started setting in for the goat lifters. Suppertime was approaching, and both boys were expected home soon. Neither of them had a fenced-in yard – nor parents – ready to house a goat. That's probably when their attention turned to me. I had a reputation as an animal lover, having had myriad pets ranging from dogs, cats and rabbits to ferrets, ducks and a horse. And my family had a fenced-in yard shielded from view by a wall of Cherry Laurel trees.

"Let's take him to Alison's!" I imagine they declared in unison. "She'd probably love to have a goat!"

So, in less time than it takes to say, "We stole a goat from a monastery," my wayward friends made the short jaunt to my house to deposit Ziggy Stardust. When they knocked on the door, beckoned me to the Suburban, and I spotted Ziggy through the rolled-down window, I became elated.

"Sure, we can put him in the backyard!" I said without a second thought. "Wait, where did y'all get him?"

"You're not going to believe this," one of my friends stammered. "We took him from the monastery at The Eternal Word Television Network. You know, the place Mother Angelica broadcasts her show from."

"What?" I sputtered? "You did what?"

As any dedicated animal lover would, though, I quickly turned my attention back to the sweet billy goat bleating from the backseat.

"Oh, come on," I said. "Bring him anyway. But we can't tell my parents where he's from. And he can only stay until y'all find somewhere else to take him. Or on second thought maybe y'all should take him back where you got him."

The decision regarding Ziggy's fate was fortunately made for us, when my sweet Mama came out to the backyard to see what we were doing and discovered Ziggy.

"Ali," she said in her South Georgia drawl. "Where did these boys get this goat and why is he foaming at the mouth?

"Uh, we picked him up off the side of a road," one of my friends fibbed, leaving out the part about the fenced-in monastery, then adding sheepishly, "I guess the cigarette butts we fed him are making him slobber."

At that moment, the stress of it all apparently got to Ziggy as he butted his head into our chimney and got one of his curved horns stuck between two bricks.

"That's it, Ali," Mama said. "You boys need to unstick that poor goat's horn and take him back where he came from!"

Realizing they were teetering on the brink of real trouble, my delinquent friends gently unstuck Ziggy's horn, and ushered him back to the Suburban where I sadly petted his head and said goodbye.

When I saw the goat lifters the next day at our Bienville hangout and asked how Ziggy had fared, they joked and said they were having a goat barbecue the next day. But they backed down quickly after seeing the look of horror on my face and said they had gently lowered him back over the EWTN fence where he trotted off toward his herd.

That was all I needed to know.

As I said before, I participated in lots of things when I was a teenager that I am sure my parents weren't proud of. In my defense, most of it was for fun and my beloved Daddy was usually in pursuit of fun himself, so I comfort myself by saying I learned from the best. Would I go back and change some things now if I could though? Yes, I would, if for no other reason than to lessen the worry I caused my parents, and because of my pesky conscience.

On the other hand, the story of Ziggy has endured ever since, and even though he did spend a short stint in my backyard, I was not a part of his lifting from the monastery. And I take comfort in my family's part in ensuring he was returned home.

I don't remember now if my parents ever knew where Ziggy came from, as I know they would have probably been pretty mad. Maybe, just maybe, they did know, and since the situation had a no-harm-no-foul ending, never let on and even used the story themselves through the years to entertain their friends.

After all, their daughter Alison didn't steal the goat. She just knew the guys who did.

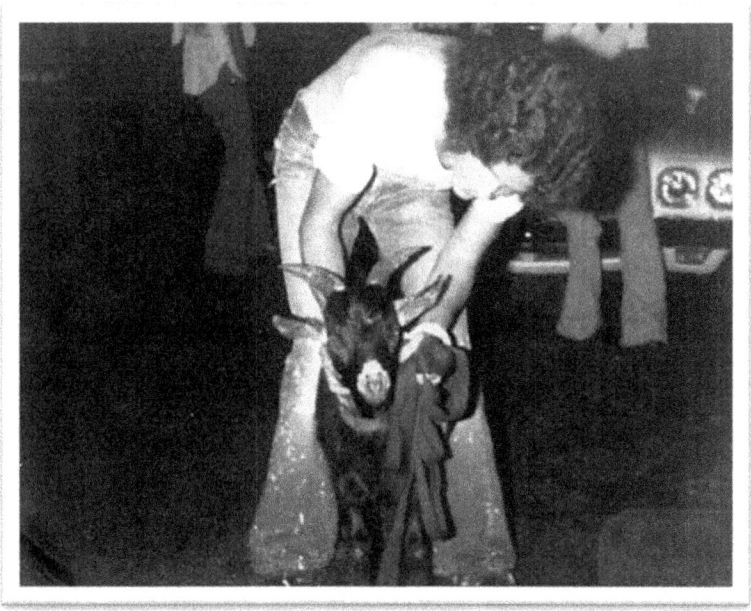

*Ziggy Stardust the billy goat pictured with a friend.*

## Where's Joe?

Daddy hustled in through the den door calling Mama's name.

"Nancy," he quivered like a fourth grader with his hand caught in the cookie jar. "We lost Joe."

It was 1972 and Mama and Daddy were in their 40s. I was 12. Cell phones didn't exist. Neither did caller ID. Gas station bathroom entrances were on the sides or backs of buildings. The drive from Destin, Florida to Birmingham took about six hours.

My father, E. Ray Large, who was an attorney and avid fisherman, was returning from a Gulf Coast little-fishing-on-a-drinking-trip vacation with buddies Carlton Wynn and Joe Adams.

"What do you mean, Ray?" Mama asked in her melodic South Georgia drawl. Mama was born and raised in Albany, Georgia (pronounced "Awolbennie" by natives). She met my father when they were students at The University of Alabama and moved with him to Birmingham after they married.

"We stopped at a gas station about an hour from the beach," Daddy said. "Joe was sleeping in the back seat. Carl and I went in to get a drink. We didn't check on Joe when we got back in the car. Heck, he was supposed to be asleep.

"A few hours later we were pulling through Jack's Hamburgers in Alabaster. Carl turned around to see if Joe wanted something to eat, and Joe wasn't there."

"Oh no, Ray," Mama said. "Where's Joe?"

"He must have gotten out at the gas station," Daddy said. "Maybe he went to the bathroom. He might still be there waiting for us to come back. I don't even remember the station name. I am not sure what to do. But I know I have to call his wife Jerri."

"Where's Carl?" Mama asked.

"I dropped Carl off at home," Daddy gulped. "He said since I was driving, the ball's in my court. What in the world am I going to say to Jerri?"

Daddy lifted the kitchen phone's harvest-gold receiver and slowly dialed Joe and Jerri's number. Tanned, unshaven, and disheveled, he looked like he was about to throw up on the kitchen floor.

Maybe it was nerves, or maybe his unfailing sense of humor. When Jerri said "Hello," Daddy started laughing and hung up.

"Ray!" Mama said. "Why did you do that?"

"How am I going to tell her I lost her husband?" Daddy asked. "I panicked."

What Daddy didn't know was that Joe had called Jerri hours earlier from the gas station payphone to say Daddy and Carl had left him and he was hitching a ride in an 18-wheeler.

"I came out of the bathroom and saw Ray and Carl pulling onto the highway," Joe told Jerri. "I started hollering and chasing them and even caught up with Ray's boat behind the car. Banged on it a couple of times before they sped off down the highway."

Jerri was already fuming. Daddy just added fuel to the fire. She recognized his machine-gun laugh before he hung up.

Our phone immediately rang back. Daddy's eyes widened to the size of large fishing bobbers.

He took a deep breath. "Hello?"

"Hello Ray," Jerri said. "Did you just call?"

Things went downhill from there.

"I am so sorry Jerri," I heard Daddy say. "Joe was asleep in the backseat when Carl and I went into the station to get a Coke. We had no idea he got out of the car."

Daddy winced under verbal face slaps.

"I know we should have turned around and checked on him," he said with sincere remorse. "But you know Carl and I would never have left Joe on purpose.

"And we didn't even stop again until we hit Alabaster," Daddy continued. "Carl turned to see if Joe wanted a hamburger and was shocked to see he wasn't there. We thought he'd been sleeping the whole time."

Daddy was silent through the rest of the call. After a couple of minutes, he gently returned the receiver to its cradle. Obviously, Jerri had dealt an earful, then hung up without giving him a chance to say goodbye.

"Joe hitched a ride with an 18-wheeler from the gas station to a station in Alabaster," Daddy said to Mama. "Jerri is picking him up in about an hour. So, the good news is, Joe got a ride. The bad news is, Jerri is furious, and I figure Joe is too.

"I don't know how I am ever going to make it up to him," he said. "I guess now I'll call Carl."

I am not sure if Daddy's and Carl's relationships with Joe ever recovered. I am certain they tried to let Joe know how bad they felt, but I suspect the five-hour drive with a stranger in an 18-wheeler had taken too big a toll for things to go back to the way they had been. All three are now gone from this life, so I don't guess I'll ever know for sure.

Daddy and Carl had countless more fishing-on-their-drinking-trips, sometimes with other friends, sometimes not. But I don't remember Joe ever going with them again.

Regardless, I know that in life's tally sheet, Daddy had a lot more check marks under the "Job-Well-Done" column than the "I-Screwed-Up" one. So, I choose to see the humor in this story.

I also choose to relish the good things I learned from my father, such as devotion to family and friends, how important it is to laugh, the value of hard work, and enjoying the time we have here, because it's over in a blink.

And there's another important lesson Daddy taught me — always check the backseat.

*Joe Adams holding his newborn son with Alison's daddy kneeling beside them in the late 1960s.*

*Alison's daddy E. Ray Large and friend Carlton Wynn doing a little fishing on a drinking trip on the Tennessee River in the early '90s.*

*Alison's cousin Billy Pickard with her daddy's friend Carlton Wynn and his wife Nancy at her daddy's 70th birthday party in the '90s.*

# Alison With One "L"

"Now everyone is going to misspell your last name too," my former husband said a few days after our wedding.

He was right.

Living with the name "Alison" spelled with one "l" has been challenging. Not earth-shatteringly hard. Not a life-or-death situation. But challenging.

The fact that I spell my name differently than most Allisons in the world crops up when least expected, like a paper cut on the tip of an index finger. It's not insurmountable, but it is pesky and irritating.

My husband had watched as time and again I would try to spell my first name more quickly than the person I was spelling it for could write or type. He was preparing me to start doubling my efforts.

"Alison with one 'l,'" I have said rapid-fire time and again just as a medical receptionist or hotel clerk moves past the first "l" onto the second, then likely onto the "i" and maybe the "s," "o," and even the "n."

Occasionally, he or she will have written or typed two "l"s followed by a "y" before realizing I was saying something they needed to hear.

"Oh, how do you spell your first name?" they look up and ask as though I haven't been spitting letters directly at — and sometimes on — them. At this point I haven't even ventured into my last name and feel like my life is a remake of the movie "Groundhog Day" with its continual time looping.

"Alison with one "l" and an "i," I say more slowly and deliberately this go-around. "A-l-i-s-o-n."

"Oh, I see," the clerk says as they draw a line — or tap a backspace key — through the misspelled version and start again.

You'd think my name was "supercalifragilisticexpialidocious," rather than Alison with one "l".

I actually prefer the way my name is spelled. It's efficient, doesn't take up more space than needed, and is phonetically easy — sounds just like it's spelled.

But all that is easily lost in the moment.

"Don't they know they are going to use up all the 'l's?" my son Zeke said once when he heard my frustration. "We are going to run out because of all the two "l" Allisons in the world."

My mind turns to a world without "l"s, and the audacity of two "l" Allisons.

"They're going to eave us not making sense when we tak," I say as though the world has in fact run out of "l"s. "And think of the dictionaries and keyboards that are going to have to be changed."

Once I was in a furniture store and a clerk approached asking if I needed help. My eyes settled on her name tag and the fact that it was imprinted with "Alison" with one "l."

"Oh my gosh," I said. "It's so nice to meet another person who spells their name correctly! My name is Alison with one 'l' too."

"I know, right?" my new friend replied. "Doesn't happen very often!"

We discussed starting a support group for one "l" Alisons, and agreed there was a need.

I never asked my parents why they chose to spell Alison with one "l". I think the more-obvious question should be asked of the parents of two "l" Allisons.

Why?

It doesn't change the pronunciation. It just adds another letter.

Zeke recently met a one "l" Alison who shares my plight, and pointed out that Allison spelled with two "l"s should be enunciated "All-i-sun."

When I married, my last name changed from "Large" to "Ketcham," and I quickly realized my husband was right. Apparently, there are a lot more "Ketchums" than there are "Ketchams." There also must be a lot of people with the last name "Ketchup."

I was exasperated when I told him about the first time I had to correct someone who spelled my new last name wrong.

"Oh, just wait," he said. "One time I was in an auto-repair shop and the woman spelled my last name 'Ketchup.'

"I told her my last name ends in 'am,' so she spelled it 'Ketchupam.'"

"Don't say any more," I said. "I give up."

# Catching Yawns

Why are yawns contagious?

We've all had it happen. Sitting around with family and friends, one person yawns and sets off a tidal wave like sports fans standing up and sitting down in a football stadium. Before you know it, the yawn has become a hot potato tossed around a room.

Power of suggestion? Maybe. Heck, I just yawned writing about yawns.

But why ONLY yawns? Why not sneezes, burps, coughs, or hiccups?

I asked my friend Danny what he thinks.

"It's a funky phenomenon," he said.

My friend Kim said she always heard it has something to do with sympathy.

"But why be sympathetic about yawns and not burps?" I asked.

"I guess because you have to have acid indigestion to make you burp?" she asked back.

There's another bodily function I have never seen anyone catch like yawns. Passing gas. Then again, that's only if we're talking about females.

Males do it all the time. But not because it's involuntary. They actually "catch" them voluntarily because they think it's funny to create a toxic mushroom cloud (which oddly smells like rancid mushrooms) by emitting disgusting noises from their rears.

But back to bodily functions people catch involuntarily from others.

For some unknown reason, I get the hiccups when I eat turkey or carrots, but never because someone in my presence hiccupped.

Two of my sons sneeze when they walk into the sunlight. One of them can even look at a lightbulb to make himself sneeze if he feels the need. Yet, I could sneeze all day long in front of them and never make either one of them sneeze — or vice versa.

But let a random stranger pass in a grocery store, yawn like a frog catching flies, make that familiar whine, and suddenly my mouth is agape and I'm at risk of sucking in a passing gnat.

The oddest example I know of someone catching a yawn happened to yours truly. Several years ago, I was driving on a two-lane country road, and midway through a yawn I realized I had just passed a yawning dog.

"What in the world?" I thought. "I just caught a yawn from a dog?"

I have gotten a lot of mileage from that story, though, making it well worth what some people might call an embarrassing incident. But I'd say it's a reflection of the fact that I love dogs, and that apparently contagious yawns are not species specific.

Maybe it's also a wink from God, to remind us that we humans are animals too.

A friend made me cringe a little though when he echoed the idea that catching yawns isn't limited to animals of the same species.

"Wonder where the dog you caught the yawn from caught it?" he said. "A possum?"

For some reason that idea just didn't sit well with me.

# Shakin' a Tower

My family loves making up words and phrases.

There's a whole heap of them that wouldn't exist if not for us. Some invented intentionally, some accidental mispronunciations of a child, but all now permanent in my vernacular.

For example, when my youngest son Johnathan was five years old, he started using the word "recolize."

"Mama, I don't recolize which shoes to wear," Johnathan said one morning, getting ready for kindergarten.

I didn't need a dictionary to know exactly what my tow-headed boy meant. Actually, I don't think a dictionary would have done much good, as I had never heard the word used before — or since — by anyone outside our family.

It's a cross between "recognize" and "realize" and to this Mama, it's brilliant.

When my cousin Patty and I were teenagers, we were riding waves in the Gulf of Mexico just off the coast of Panama City, Florida. Two silly girls, soaking up the sun, talking about boys, Peter Frampton's live album, and who just jumped higher over the last wave.

"Hey, let's make up our own form of Pig Latin," Patty said during a wave lull. "Swap the first sounds of two words in a sentence."

The world of made-up words suddenly became our oyster. Little did we realize one of the phrases we were about to create would stay with us the rest of our lives.

"Instead of saying 'take a shower,'" Patty said. "Let's say 'shake a tower.'"

I haven't taken a shower since that day. But I have shaken many a tower.

When my older son Zeke was four years old, we were in the kitchen, and I told his Dad I was heading upstairs. His father was familiar with — and had adopted some of — the phrases Patty and I created on that beach trip all those years prior.

"I am going up to shake a tower," I said, not giving a second thought to the fact that Zeke hadn't yet learned to play musical chairs with the letters in words.

Moments later, I heard the bathroom door creak open, and slid back the shower door to Zeke leaning his head in with tears streaming down his face.

"Oh Buddy," I said. "What's wrong?"

"You said you were coming up here to shake a tower, and I wanted to see," he said.

Lesson learned. Gauge your audience before you go messing with the English language. And for Pete's sake, don't cangle a darrot like shaking a tower in a small bathroom if you aren't going to deliver.

"Sweet boy, Mama was just kidding when I said I was going to shake a tower," I ineptly explained to my son. "I meant I was taking a shower."

A couple of years later I was able to adequately describe to him how the term "shake a tower" came to be.

"Aunt Patty and I started talking wackbards while we were widing raves at the beach," I said.

"Oh, I get it," Zeke replied, immediately adding "talking wackbards" and "widing raves" and to his own vernacular.

My husband enjoyed playing with language too. I don't think I ever heard him say "aluminum foil" the way most folks do. To him, it was "al-you-men-ee-um" foil. As in "I am going to wrap those steaks in al-you-men-ee-um foil after I take them off the grill."

When we would get up at sunrise to fish, he and I both said we were rising at the "dack of crawn."

Two words I say and write regularly are "absotively" and "posilutely," more-commonly known as "absolutely" and "positively."

I don't remember how or when I mangled those two, but the kie is dast.

So go ahead and ask me if there's a better way to kin a skat when it comes to language.

My answer?

"Tarn dootin'!"

*Alison's older son Zeke around the time he learned the art of talking wackbards.*

# The Tooth Fairy?

I awoke to a parent's worst nightmare when my five-year-old son poked my shoulder as I was lying in bed early one Saturday morning to tell me the tooth fairy had been a no-show.

"Uh, she probably knew your friends spent the night and was afraid she'd wake them up," I responded clumsily, attempting to cover my inexcusable oversight.

Truth be known, I had collapsed the night before after keeping up for hours with three five-year-olds. Now, the sun was barely peeking over the horizon, I was drop-dead exhausted, and suddenly scrambling in my semi-awake state to cover my tracks (or lack thereof).

My son sensed my hesitation.

"Mama, you're the tooth fairy, aren't you?" he lisped through a gaping hole in his smile.

I was in no way ready to spill the beans and single handedly ruin this slice of childhood magic for him. Never mind extinguishing the enjoyment I got from being said fairy. Nope, I quickly mustered the best no-coffee-yet follow-up I could.

"Now Buddy," I started slowly. "How could I be the tooth fairy AND be your mother? I'd have to fly all over the world every night, collecting teeth and leaving money under kids' pillows. Then be home in time to fix you and your brother's breakfast."

I held my breath and said a prayer my response wasn't too flimsy for him to swallow.

"Oh, ok," he said after a moment's hesitation, spinning on his sock-covered heel and heading out the bedroom door, satisfied with my logic — or lack thereof.

"Whew," I thought, happy to have staved off the inevitable for at least another tooth or two and swearing to myself — and the tooth fairy — it would never happen again.

Now don't even get me started on Santa Claus.

*Alison's younger son Johnathan around the time he became skeptical about the tooth fairy.*

# Doppelgänger

I have a familiar face.

Blessing or curse, it's a fact.

I would run out of fingers, toes, and strands of hair counting how many times strangers have asked "Don't I know you?"

Sometimes it's flattering. Other times it's not. At times I feel like a blond-haired blue-eyed woman devoid of any unique features.

I also have been compared to famous people for as far back as I can remember, leading me to wonder if we humans have been cloned after all.

"You are a dead-ringer for Goldie Hawn," I heard over and over when I was single-digit young, and she was a regular in the 1960s comedy "Laugh In."

"You look exactly like Florence Henderson," played frequently in my '60s and '70s soundtrack. (Think mother in the sitcom "The Brady Bunch.")

Fast forward to the '80s.

"It's amazing how much you look like Meg Ryan," I heard time and time (and time) again. (Think "When Harry Met Sally.")

I used to joke that when I grew up, I wanted to be actress Betty White (who died in 2021 at 99 years old). But so help me, if someone tells me I look like Betty's surviving twin, I am drawing the curtain and closing up shop.

In the '70s and '80s, I heard more than once I looked just like a two "l" Allison who went to a local Catholic school with several of my friends. My small world shrank when I met her in the '90s.

I had seen her picture and recognized her immediately.

"Hey, are you Allison?" I asked.

"Yes," she answered quizzically. She obviously had never heard of me. After I told her about all the comparisons, we both stepped back, and looked at each other up and down.

"I don't see it," I said.

"Me either," she replied.

Go figure.

In the '80s my sister swore she saw my twin at the popular Birmingham pub named Dugan's.

"I almost walked up to her," Lisa said. "But I finally realized she wasn't you."

Another time I was in an elevator, the doors opened, a lady stepped in, and said "Don't I know you?"

I asked the worn-out list of questions. "Did we meet in high school?" "College?" "Our kids' schools?" "Work?" "Through my crazy friend Elise?"

"I guess not," I concluded when she answered "No" to every question. "But you're not the first person who has asked. Guess I have a familiar face."

Right then, the elevator doors opened, and another lady stepped in.

"Don't I know you?" she asked.

"I don't think so," I said, stepping out on my floor.

I looked back at the first lady.

"I rest my case," I shrugged.

# Uncle Bill

The buck started stopping here several years ago when my two uncles and last living aunt all died within a few months of each other. Even though I was in my 50s at the time, I had always loved knowing there were older family members to turn to. My Aunt Joyce passed away many years earlier. And Mama and Daddy had died years before on two of the most-heartbreaking days of my life.

This meant they were all gone.

The fact really hit home when my sons and I came back from Uncle Bill's funeral in Atlanta. Uncle Bill died of natural causes at 90 years old. He was a World War II veteran who was deeply entrenched in some of its bloodiest battles. Yet Uncle Bill was also a man I never heard speak a harsh word to — or about — anyone. He loved his family, his country and writing country music. He was kind, spoke with a melodic Southern drawl, and had a sense of humor that could sneak up on you like a stealthy lion intent on capturing its prey.

Tom Brokaw was right when named his book — and coined the phrase — "The Greatest Generation." These family members were of that generation. They were tough and wise individuals who learned the hard lessons of the Great Depression, and who eagerly answered the call a few years later when their country beckoned them to war.

My father, E. Ray Large, served in the U.S. Navy in the South Pacific. My uncle, James Willard Large, served in the U.S. Air Force. And my Uncle Bill Pickard served in the U.S. Army. I will always be immensely proud of each of them, as well as their wives, children, and other relatives who loved them so.

Here's what I wrote when my two sons and I returned to Birmingham from Uncle Bill's funeral:

Spent all last week in Atlanta with my kids and cousins, following the death of my precious Uncle Bill. Throughout the week we reminisced, laughed, cried, went through boxes of old pictures, wrote Uncle Bill's obituary, laid out the program for his funeral, visited with extended family and old friends, ate, slept and breathed our memories.

We also gingerly picked through Uncle Bill's tie tacks, cufflinks, watches, pocketknives, dog tags, and war medals, longing to be able to grasp something that would make reality untrue, and the pain go away.

But through it all, we had each other's support, and the mission of providing my uncle a sendoff worthy of a World War II veteran who heard the initial shots launching the Battle of the Bulge, and who participated in the brutal combat on Omaha Beach on Day 2 of the Normandy Invasion.

We accomplished that mission. Two young soldiers and a bugler playing "Taps" helped honor my uncle's service in the graveside portion of his funeral. A bagpiper wearing a kilt and cap and playing "How Great Thou Art" and "Amazing Grace" added a moving touch since a large portion of our ancestry is Scottish.

Most poignant is the fact that dear Uncle Bill's four grandsons and two great nephews (my sons), ranging in age from 11 to 19 carried his casket. And after they placed it on the straps above the grave, these young men all stood tall, as soldiers at attention would, with tears streaming down their faces.

Yesterday we loaded up and came back home to Birmingham to pick up where we left off seven days ago. And it is only now, when we're called upon to carry on in my uncle's absence, that the tears for me keep coming.

He was the final living member of that generation of my family, as my wonderful Uncle Jim and Aunt Liz have both passed away since then. And I am feeling a profound sense of how fleeting this life truly is. I hope and pray that I never take for granted that the people I love know that I love them.

The generation of my family now missing here on earth always made me feel safe and cared for. I want to keep that feeling in their honor, and I pray I am the rock for the next generation that the previous one always was for me.

Rest in peace my dear Uncle Bill, until we all meet again.

*Alison's Uncle Bill when he was a 19-year-old World War II soldier*

# Fruit Flies

They're winged. They're pesky. They're irritating. They're probably also really dirty, since they're attracted to rotting fruit and unsanitary sink drains.

They sometimes make appearances on bathroom mirrors and lighted cell-phone screens in dark rooms when you're playing virtual solitaire.

They're fruit flies. And as many times as I have seen them in my home — and countless others — I don't know much about them, like why they appear so suddenly and multiply like tiny flying rabbits.

No sooner do I notice one zipping around my fruit bowl like a microscopic drone scouting for brown spots, than a swarm ensues as though there was a clone experiment gone awry in the trash can.

An elderly lady recently corrected me when I told her I was battling fruit flies in my kitchen and bathroom.

"No honey," she said. "The ones in the bathroom are sewer flies."

"What the heck?" I pondered. "They come in different versions, one of which originates in the portal to the final resting place for human feces?"

Now that IS nasty.

And I am not a nasty person, nor do I keep a nasty home. Sure, the banana at the bottom of the bunch might have gotten over-soft and developed a few bruises by the time I noticed it was no longer edible.

And I'll admit, I don't pour baking soda and white vinegar down my drains on a regular basis like I should. I guess I am more of a hit-or-miss out-of-sight-out-of-mind kinda gal when it comes to drains and pipes.

But the elderly woman's declaration piqued my interest, so I decided to see if there are such things as sewer flies — not to be confused with fruit flies — and learn the difference between the two.

While researching, I discovered yet a third flying varmint I could one day have to deal with — fungus gnats. Yay!

"Just what I need," I thought, "another interloper taking up airspace around me, making my head bob and weave and causing me to leave handprints on mirrors eradicating them the old-fashioned way."

A quick online search revealed there are indeed such unspeakables as sewer flies. Here's a few Wikipedia high points:

"Drain flies, sink flies, filter flies, sewer flies, or sewer gnats, is a family of true flies."

"Are there fake flies?" I wonder.

"Some genera have short, hairy bodies and wings giving them a 'furry' moth-like appearance, hence one of their common names, 'moth flies'," Wikipedia continues.

And on contravermin.com I found:

"We do not come into contact with (sewer flies) very much," it read. "Their larvae are mainly found in sewage-treatment beds."

So even though there are such things as sewer flies, the ones in my bathroom must have been dazed-and-confused fruit flies since they looked nothing like microscopic moths (that I could tell) and I live nowhere near sewage-treatment beds (that I know of).

I also learned why fruit flies are so prolific. According to the University of Kentucky College of Agriculture, Food and Environment site:

"A single rotting potato or onion forgotten at the back of a closet, or fruit-juice spillage under a refrigerator can breed thousands of fruit flies," it says. "Given the opportunity, they will lay about 500 eggs."

Awesome! Pile it on!

As I am writing this at a corner table in Starbucks, I am becoming increasingly aware of a handful of tiny flies darting around my iPad screen.

And I am wondering if they hatched on an apple – or maybe in a toilet.

Here's the delightful information I gathered about fungus gnats from the University of Maryland Extension site:

"Fungus gnats are tiny, black flies that are commonly seen around lamps and windows," it said. "The larvae breed in moist soil, primarily in potted plants containing soil rich in organic matter."

"That's not so bad," I thought. "Right now I don't have an abundance of indoor plants, so I probably won't have to deal with those."

I continue reading the UM site.

"They can also breed in drains."

"Dammit," I thought. "I'm stopping on the way home for a big box of baking soda and a jug of vinegar!"

# Online Dating

As my Uncle Bill would say when he was a widower dating in his 60s, "Women are looking for their knight in shining armor, and at this age we all got a little tarnish on us."

Update: Since writing this chapter, I fortunately have met a man that I am crazy about and who feels the same about me. However, I went through many years after my divorce single and hoping to meet "Mr. Right." So, I am keeping this chapter intact as I think some might relate. By the way, my new fella and I met through a mutual friend who introduced us simply as that — friends. I guess what they say is right – it happens when you're not looking.

It sucks.

I could just leave it at that, and anyone who has ever dipped their pointer finger into the online-dating pool will understand without another word.

But for those fortunate souls who have not chosen between swatting left and swiping right, here's the deal.

I never imagined I would be single and dating in my 60s, but I still believe I have plenty of love to give. I've tasted the sweetness of a good relationship and would love to love again. There was a time — not so long ago — when I held a man I adored in the proverbial palm of my hand. My ex-husband was a person who loved me unconditionally and about whom I felt the same.

But then a pesky "condition" began cracking the foundation of our "unconditionalism," first peeking into our lives like a nosy neighbor peering over the back fence, eventually growing bolder, passing through the gate into our yard, and busting through the front door yelling "I am here! The elephant in the room! You can't ignore me anymore!"

I never stopped loving him, but the once rock-solid foundation which made our lives so enjoyable, grew irreparably damaged. A few years after our divorce, he died of cancer, and at times I grieve what might have been if we had stayed together and weathered the storms.

But life often charts its own course, and now I sometimes find myself hoping I'm on the cusp of finding my last true love by staring into a phone screen and making blind choices. All while thinking the odds of nailing down a second once-in-a-lifetime relationship is like aiming a bow-and-arrow backward over my shoulder at a bullseye I need a periscope to see.

Dating at this age feels like dumping the pieces of two jigsaw puzzles on a table and simultaneously trying to separate them while also piecing each together.

Not that I haven't met my share of nice men.

I've been out with musicians, writers, attorneys, engineers, policemen, business owners, salesmen, an electrician and a farmer. Some were widowers with kids at home. Others were divorced empty nesters. Still others had never been married and had no children.

I've shared meals, drinks and/or coffee with extroverts, introverts, military veterans, fishermen, hunters, tennis players, pickleball enthusiasts, cyclists, runners, and more.

I have laughed, cried, gotten mad, and felt sad over the outcomes of some of those dates. And I have taken long breaks from dating altogether. But my optimistic side keeps whispering "maybe this time."

I have dated men who would have "put a ring on it," if I had been receptive. And there have been those I could potentially have said "yes" to, who never asked.

So far "never the twain shall meet" as the saying goes.

A good friend who is also treading water in the dating pool has a hilarious habit of nicknaming her "suitor of the month" alliteration style. Take for example the college professor she thought she was dating exclusively until she found at a girls-night-out dinner that he had also been courting a friend of one of the women at the table.

And just like that, "Textbook Tom" became "Two-Timing Toupee Tom." (Based on his bangs, we're pretty sure he wears a hairpiece.)

Then there was the retired federal agent she went out with until he ghosted her, and we later found out was married.

She called him "Detective Dan."

Following her lead, I coined the name "Jammin' Jeff" for a musician I went out with — who had played bass for a popular 1970s Southern Rock Band — until I realized he had a case of hypochondria, he (thankfully) broke it off with me for a lame reason, and I changed his name to "Jerky Jeff."

But before you get to the going-out, giving-'em-a-name stage, you first have to hurdle the online profile. Let's just say at the end of many swipe sessions, there are more smears off the left edge of my screen than the right.

Here's a few of the reasons.

A profile picture of a man with a dead animal. No offense to hunting enthusiasts, but if the best you have features you smiling as you prop up the lifeless head of a creature you just slaughtered, we're not a match.

Likewise for dead animal heads on walls. Especially if one is centered behind the potential suitor's head. Nothing screams "This guy hates animals AND skipped the photography class on composition" like deer antlers appearing to emerge from his noggin.

And I can't swipe left fast enough when a man's profile pic is of his shirtless reflection in a dirty bathroom mirror with a plastic shower curtain in the background. 'Nuff said.

There are books, podcasts, blogs, videos, Facebook groups, and TV shows devoted to finding a match via online dating. Makes me long for the days when a boy asked if he could call me at a certain time and I was sitting by my princess phone when he did.

Sometimes I compare online dating to choosing items from a salad bar. And truth be known, I have become a picky eater.

So, for example, while deciding what to put on my plate, I figure even if I skip the wilted broccoli, there's plenty of fresh peppers, plump grape tomatoes, and dried cranberries on down the line.

Similarly, even if I swipe left on the profile of a handsome accountant because he looks drunk in one of his pictures or because I am not enamored with numbers, I figure surely a kind-looking and sober veterinarian, or a tall, distinguished fellow-writer will pop up next.

On the other hand, (as I once heard in an old movie) "there aren't that many shopping days left until Christmas," so I might need to accept at this stage, none of us — including me — is as fresh as we once were.

And maybe I should just give that wilted broccoli a second look or scrape off a bit of that tarnish to reveal the somewhat-shiny armor underneath.

Or maybe I should just be content and grateful I have known true love. And rest easy in the love of my kids and grandchildren.

I'll let you know how it goes.

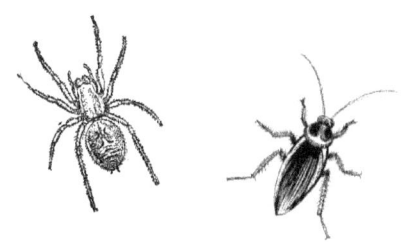

## Spiders vs. Roaches

I have never been a fan of spiders.

Fortunately, over the years my razor-sharp fear has worn to dull displeasure, but I still don't celebrate their presence. Nor do I feel guilty flattening them with a heel or dousing them with Raid.

"He's just trying to make his way like you and me," my cousin Susan said recently as I headed toward a slow-moving dark spot on the wall, shoe in hand.

"Well, he picked the wrong way today," I responded, smushing him with my sneaker.

Not all people have the aversion I do to spiders. Some claim roaches are more detestable, as though we are in a heated game of insect poker — the winner holding cards emblazoned with pics of the-most-hated bug.

"Oh, roaches are worse than spiders," a friend declared recently between coffee sips, one-upping my arachnid aversion. "You do know if we have a worldwide nuclear war, roaches and rats will be the only creatures that survive."

"First off, if we have a worldwide nuclear war, who cares what survives?" I quipped. "And what does a roach's ability to withstand fallout have to do with whether or not I should hate them more than spiders?"

It is true roaches carry myriad germs making them irrepressibly disgusting, but they aren't vicious and don't bite. Their lives are pretty one dimensional. If they have a mind at all, it's got a single track — finding their next meal.

Roaches make beelines to food, whether hamburger patties on a platter, chicken bones at the bottom of a trash bag, or spent banana slices frisbeed under the hutch by a toddler.

They are sneaky, though, preferring to come out at night when lights are low and no one's around over diving into a gravy boat at the Thanksgiving table.

Spiders, on the other hand, are sinister planners. They're the Nazis of the bug world, never missing a chance to inflict harm and suffering. Spiders will lie in wait like a crocodile under the surface of a lake waiting for a deer to lean in for a drink.

How many times have I heard horror stories of brown recluses hiding in the toe of a shoe, poised to sink in fangs and release poison into a bloodstream? And how many times have I seen pictures of decaying flesh in the wake of such a bite?

My friend Patrick was bitten by a brown recluse once while he was sleeping. Over the course of two weeks, he went from waking with an itchy spot on his hand to developing congestive heart and kidney failure.

"The doctors thought the venom got into my bloodstream and went to my heart, kidneys and liver," Patrick said. "I still have congestive heart failure years later.

"I avoid spiders like the plague. I hate them all."

Unlike Patrick, I have never gone toe-to-toe with a brown recluse, but I do remember encountering a black widow under a rock I flipped in 1994 while planting pansies.

I almost gave up gardening. Thought seriously about selling the house and moving.

Conversely, a roach in the garden would give me pause and I would probably kill it if I could, but I wouldn't call a moving truck.

My father was a bustling attorney, building a successful personal-injury practice when I was young. I didn't understand back then why Daddy sometimes provided short, curt answers to my ponderings.

I now realize he had more important things on his mind than whether caught-and-released bass might associate eating with pain and become anorexic, or whether I truly had a spider phobia.

"Fish eat other fish, with fins and bones included," Daddy said. "You're not hurting the fish you catch. Just keep fishing, Alison."

"And it's not good to have phobias."

Case closed.

Recently, when one my sons Johnathan and I were visiting cousins on their 128-acre farm in east Georgia, I happily volunteered to clean windows in preparation for more guests.

I did away with my fair share of eight-leggers in window corners that day, delighting in annihilating several waiting on unsuspecting moths or crickets.

While washing panes and listening to John Denver singing "Country Roads," I recalled once hearing a statistic about how many spiders there are per square acre. I pulled out my phone and turned to the internet for answers, where I read there are an estimated million spiders per acre of land on earth, with an estimated three million per acre in the tropics.

"That settles it," I thought. "No more pining to go to the tropics."

"Y'all, guess what?" I called to my son and cousins, "There are 128-million spiders on this farm. And if you think that number is inflated, remember many live in trees and bushes."

"That's comforting," I thought. "I would rather doubt the number than know there are millions of spiders in trees and bushes around me."

My beliefs about roaches and spiders, oddly, were put to the test a few days after I thought I had put writing this chapter to bed.

I walked into my freshly cleaned kitchen to pour a cup of coffee, and perched atop the sink rim was a medium-size roach. I calmly unwound a couple of paper towels, smushed him with my hand, and deposited him into the trash.

Thirty minutes later, I stepped out of the shower, reached for a towel and immediately felt something move under my hand.

I looked down to see a harmless cellar spider between my fingers and let out a yell loud enough to scare neighbors in surrounding states. I slung the towel, so the spider landed in a leggy heap on the tile floor a few feet away. I grabbed a wad of toilet paper, hit him using my hand like a mallet, and slammed him into the toilet, whimpering the entire time.

There was a fresh chill in the air that day. I guess those critters were just trying to find their way to warmer surroundings.

Unfortunately for them, they chose the wrong way.

# Catching Up To Do

*An ode to our family's Yorkshire Terrier, Hershey, who died a few years ago at 14. She had been part of our family from the time she was six weeks old. If you don't believe animals go to heaven, we'll just have to agree to disagree.*

I sure hope that heaven welcomes animals,
    And we can understand what it is they have to say.
I'd love to ask sweet Hershey what she's been up to,
    'Cause we sure got some catching up to do.

I'd ask her if her life with us was happy,
    And if I'd done anything to make her mad.
I'd invite her without fear to gently clear the air,
    So we could focus on all the good times we'd had.

I'd want to know if she'd hated wearing a collar,
    And then on top of that a leash.
I'd remind her of first the time I took them off her,
    Because I knew she always wanted to roam free.

From that point on I rarely put them on her,
    Unless that put her at all in harm's way.
Like when we were way down in Tampa, Florida,
    Where big hawks circled overhead each day.

I suspect she'd talk about our many car rides,
    Her silky ears flapping in the wind.
She'd say thanks for always rolling down the window,
    Even when the cold and rain came pouring in.

She probably thank me for the scraps we fed her,
    She never liked dry gravel anyway.
She'd say she appreciated eating like a carnivore,
    'Cause real meat beats kibbles any ol' day.

She'd also say she loved being a Mama,
    And thanks for arranging for her and Boudreaux's date.
So a few months later those precious pups would come from her,
    And make her life so much more than great.

And when the time came for her to wean her babies,
>    I am sure she'd say she was glad that we stepped in.
Instead of selling those bundles of joy to strangers,
>    We gave them each to the loving homes of friends.

I'd tell her a big part of me died that Easter,
>    When I awoke to find her cozy in her bed.
And I knew my life was changing — not for the better,
>    When I called her name and she didn't lift her head.

I'd thank her for the white dove she sent to greet me,
>    Under the overpass on the way to the funeral home.
I'd say from then on her ashes were always with me,
>    And also her precious paw print etched in stone.

I'd thank her for all the years she gave me,
>    And to my boys that she helped me to raise.
For always being a calm and steady presence,
>    Even during some of our darkest days.

And then I'd find some crystal-clear running water,
>    Whether a creek, a lake, or maybe just a stream.
And my girl and I'd keep talking and strolling toward it,
>    And I'd thank God for answering my dreams.

Yes, I sure hope that heaven welcomes animals,
    And we can understand what it is they need to say.
I'd love to ask sweet Hershey what she's been up to,
    'Cause we sure got some catching up to do.

*Alison's beloved family dog Hershey.*

*Hershey smiling over her passel of four newborn puppies.*

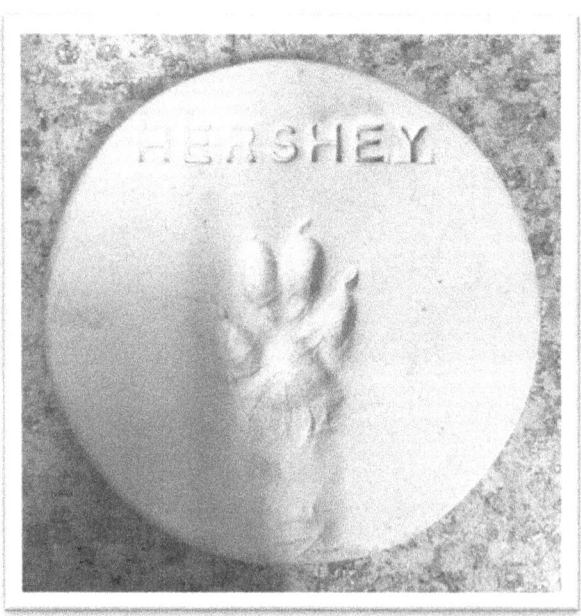

*Hershey's paw print made by the funeral home.*

# Author Bio

Alison Large Ketcham is an award-winning Southern writer with a unique ability to bring stories to life. A former newspaper reporter and editor who grew up in a family of storytellers, Alison knows how to engage readers and leave them wanting more. She delights in laughter, family, animals, the outdoors, card games, honesty, love, and more. She's carried many of the stories included in this, her first book, in her heart and head for a long time.

Growing up in the South, Alison learned the gift of storytelling early on from lots of relatives, including her father and two uncles. She and many of her cousins have kept that gift alive, although Alison is the first to collect her stories in book form.

Raised in a suburb of Birmingham, Alabama during the racially turbulent 1960s, Alison learned valuable lessons from her parents who instilled that we all deserve respect regardless of race, skin color, or any other of the traits that so divided so many at the time.

She hopes that a couple of the stories in this collection reflect the depth of that belief planted so long ago, while others leave readers laughing, smiling, and recognizing that sometimes truth is more interesting than fiction.

## Thank You

To my kids and step kids, Zeke, Johnathan, Putter and Beanie, as well as cousins, other relatives and friends who have heard me talk about publishing my first book for longer than I like to admit. I'll always be grateful for your encouragement and cheerleading.

Thank you also to Benny for your tireless love and support.

I love you all.

www.ingramcontent.com/pod-product-compliance
Lightning Source LLC
Chambersburg PA
CBHW050916160426
43194CB00011B/2433